S0-ABR-717

norman

gorbaty

to

honor

my

people

judaica

This publication accompanies the exhibition
Norman Gorbaty: To Honor My People

Exhibition dates:

Thomas J. Walsh Art Gallery
Quick Center for the Arts
Diana Mille, Ph.D., Director
Fairfield University
Fairfield, Connecticut
January 27th - March 27th, 2011

Norman Gorbaty: Works in Dialogue

Exhibition Dates:
The Bellarmine Museum of Art
Fairfield University
Fairfield, Connecticut
Jill Deupi, J.D., Ph.D., Director
January 27th - March 28th, 2011

Curator: Ben Gorbaty
Book Design: Andrew Patapis Design, New York, NY
Design Assistant: Michelle LaRocca
Design Consultant: Norman Gorbaty
Archivist: Shelley Kaiser-Gorbaty
Printer: Laserwave, Inc., New Brunswick, NJ
Photo Credits: Chuck Kintzing, Guenter Knop, Shelley Kaiser-Gorbaty

ISBN: 978-0-615-39348-3
LCCN: 2010934971

Publication accompanying the exhibitions held at the Thomas J. Walsh Art Gallery, Quick Center for the Arts, Fairfield University, Fairfield, CT, January 27th - March 27th 2011 and The Bellarmine Museum of Art, Fairfield University, Fairfield, CT, January 27th – March 28th 2011.

Published by North American Thought Combine, Inc. 2010

www.schneersoncenter.org

North American Thought Combine, Incorporated

A

Hartsen

Dank

A

Heartfelt

Thank

You

My unbelievable son Ben and his wife Shelley, for their neverending commitment to make this happen. I cautioned them — argued with them to not take on the task of making me known — to no avail. I would like to forget the bitter clashes, the arguments, but they too are part of the working experience. If not for them you would not be reading this book and experiencing my work. I would still be hiding my light under a bushel. It is hard for me to outwardly express my love for them, but I do so, for changing my life.

To Diane Mille, Ph.D., Ellen M. Umansky, Ph.D., and Philip Eliasoph, Ph.D., whose sight into what I am about was so beautifully expressed in their essays.

Joy, my late "old beauty," for having endured me for over fifty years. For taking care of the life tasks that would have given me less time to "do" things. For having supported me in the doing and in her near successful effort to make me a mensch. For her love and support. I love her still.

My daughter Lisa and her husband Bill Haldane and my grandchildren Becky and Lizzie, for being there to help fill the void when Joy left us. Their stability, inclusion, concern and love kept me "a part of." I love and am proud of them as I would like to think they are of me.

Andrew Patapis, who worked with me, side by side for a lifetime in graphic design. We've shared the doing. His stability and calmness of character has sustained me. He is both a brother and a son to me. His contribution in doing this catalog made it happen!

Chuck Kintzing, master photograhper and designer, who when asked, unhesitatingly gave his all in making this project happen. A true friend.

Hariet Eckstein, whose encouragement to overcome self-doubt, whose faith in me has given me the strength and confidence to continue the doing. You were the rock that kept me going.

ng

Norman Gorbaty: A Modern Master Of Judaica

by Diana Mille, Ph.D.

Diana Mille has been director of the Thomas J. Walsh Art Gallery and Adjunct Professor of Art History at Fairfield University since 1997. Dr. Mille received her Ph.D. from CUNY Graduate Center, NYC in 1993 specializing in 19th and 20th century art and criticism. Her research and publications focus on the 19th century tonal school and on a variety of multicultural topics in contemporary art. At Fairfield, her courses include Modern, Contemporary Art & Criticism, African American Art and History of Photography. By offering a wide range of diverse and multicultural programming, Dr. Mille has envisioned the gallery as both a hands-on laboratory for Fairfield University students and faculty as well as a venue for educational outreach programming for students and adults in the community. In 2009, she completed her MA in Marriage and Family Therapy at Fairfield University. Dr. Mille believes that her studies have further enhanced her teaching and communications skills with her students and gallery interns on many levels.

As with all great art revealing unique and creative genius, the sculptures and drawings of Norman Gorbaty deliberately convey the intentions of their maker. In Gorbaty's case, his intentions are to inquire with a questioning soul, to see with an open mind, and to interpret and describe with a passionate heart. While Gorbaty's sculptures and drawings suggest both ancient and modern Judaic narratives, a carefully thought out "staccato-like" process, and an aesthetic that many would argue is "to die for," the artist humbly maintains that he is simply a *picture doer.*

In the course of preparing my essay through dialogue and observation, however, I discovered my sympathies lie, instead, with the response of one Rabbi to the artist's self-perception of being simply a *doer of pictures*, "*You create Norman, and that is godlike.*" Without a doubt, Gorbaty knows how to create, and brilliantly at that. The artist demonstrates with conviction the kind of courage and passion in "taking risks" with forms, shapes and symbols which compete with the likes of artists such as Gauguin, Cezanne, Picasso and Matisse. Gorbaty's works demonstrate, for example, — and even challenge in some cases — the highly complex, fragmented and psychologically-charged narratives first proposed by these early modernists.

A major methodology that presents itself in Gorbaty's work is that of a creator who recapitulates in his mind the stories and perceptions from his family of origin, his tribe of Judaic culture and even from those outside this culture and then collects imagery and means — largely drawing and movement — to bring the narrative to life. The works that comprise "To Honor My People" — currently on view at the Thomas J. Walsh Art Gallery at Fairfield University — are a memorial to acquaint fellow Jews and non-Jews alike with significant meaning which is intended to last.

As Gorbaty explains, "*I have always been a doer of images. The mystery is in the doing. In all my doing, Jewish themes keep emerging. Not unusual in that I am a Jew. These images speak to the suffering of my people, and the contributions they have made to mankind. I make visual statements to save from anonymity those who have suffered for being Jews throughout history: to never forget the road we Jews are traveling.*"

However, in his "*doing*," the artist also suggests that the works he creates are equipped with secondary stories which invite a further reading and interpretation. Since there were many different authors presenting in the Bible, Gorbaty also feels that there can be more than one interpretation for each single biblical account. One such example can be found in Gorbaty's *Peniel* — the biblical story traditionally interpreted as Jacob wrestling with an Angel. According to Gorbaty, this image, however, could as easily signify an internal struggle — "*man fighting against himself*."

Gorbaty's journey, which speaks to the suffering of his people, continues in sculptures such as *Struma* and *4856 (In memoriam)*. *Struma*, a vessel which set sail in 1942 from Europe with 769 Jews who were seeking asylum in Palestine, was refused entry into Turkey. With the exception of one child, the vessel's remaining passengers were left helpless to drift under the most inhumane conditions. The imagery and meaning in *4856 (In memoriam)* instead, refers to a much earlier holocaust in world history — the first crusade — and brings to our attention the fact that "*Little mention is made of the destruction of Jewish communities throughout Europe, especially along the Rhine, where more than 14,000 Jews were killed by peasants and crusaders on their way to Jerusalem for just being Jews.*"

It is the artist's process that also further engages the viewer in a continuous, yet somewhat dichotomous dialogue. Although the biblical themes present in Gorbaty's *Creation Series* are quite specific in their imagery (e.g., *Creation of Adam*, *Creation of Eve*, *Eden*, *Temptation*, *Expulsion*, *Birth of Cain)*, the artist reminds us that he really just intended these works as "*really points of view which are never finished*." Many of Gorbaty's larger sculptural works, for example, begin as brief sketches, thumbnails, scribbles — only to take the shape of monumental carvings many years later. For example, The Animals –the first sculpture in Gorbaty's *Creation Series* — was begun by the artist at the time of his son Ben's Bar Mitzvah, while the final work, *The Expulsion*, was not completed until twenty-five years later.

Gorbaty also reminds us of the aesthetic and technical similarities between his process of carving and drawing — a delicacy of heavenly lines and light that truly honors the viewer (as seen in his drawings entitled *Shul* and *Shtettel*). Carving in bas relief was for Gorbaty a very similar process as to drawing — using a chisel instead of a pencil, pen or brush. Whether the lines are expressed in two or three dimensions — cut softly into the bass or walnut surfaces or gently gliding along the surface of his drawings, they elicit the poetry of an experienced and emotional tracing that relies on light and shadow to define the image. As the artist himself admits, "*Drawing for me is basic to all forms of the visual arts. In doing drawing one becomes a magician symbolically defining three dimensional form in two dimensions. The mark, the line, darkness and light are units of language, as is the word or grammar for communicating feelings, ideas and thought.*"

It is fair to say that Gorbaty is sort of a magician in all that he does. The artist's career in general has been one of constant dichotomy and motion, for example, — remembering that Gorbaty's sculptures and drawings were created against the backdrop of a 50-year career in advertising and graphic design. Gorbaty studied art at Amherst College, Yale University School of Art and Architecture and the Yale Norfolk Summer Arts School, Gorbaty worked consistently in the area of graphic art — at James Eng Associates, L.W. Frolich, Benton and Bowles Advertising, as an adjunct professor of Advanced Graphic Design at Cooper Union and opened his own graphic design studio in 1968. In the end, however, whether designing, sculpting or drawing Gorbaty makes his marks, and those marks inform him where to go next until he imbues them with a life of their own. Like a magician, the artist makes things come alive. His images are constantly moving around us and we sense their motion through the differing perspectives which become our world and our works.

"*It is (the) doing of the work that I am about. I am fascinated by the motion around us and often try to capture this in my work. There is movement in life as we "do" it. Everything moves. Images are constantly in motion. This movement combines with our differing perspectives of an image to create unique experiences that I artistically explore.*" (Norman Gorbaty)

Art As Remembrance

by Ellen M. Umansky, Ph.D.

Ellen M. Umansky is the Carl and Dorothy Bennett Professor of Judaic Studies at Fairfield University in Fairfield, Connecticut, a position she has held since September of 1994. She received her B.A. degree in Philosophy from Wellesley College, her Master of Arts degree in Religion from Yale University, and her Ph.D. degree in Religion from Columbia University. She is the author of many essays, book chapters, encyclopedia articles, and books including From Christian Science to Jewish Science: Spiritual Healing and American Jews, *published by Oxford University Press in 2005 and the co-edited* Four Centuries of Jewish Women's Spirituality: A Sourcebook *(1992; second revised and expanded edition, 2009). She is currently working on a new book, focusing on Judaism, feminism, liberalism, and God.*

The Carl and Dorothy Bennett Center for Judaic Studies at Fairfield University is honored to bring Norman Gorbaty to the University campus in conjunction with the Walsh Gallery's two month exhibition of many of his Jewish-themed works. On February 9, 2011, Norman will deliver the biannual Samuel and Bettie Roberts Memorial Lecture in Jewish Art. This lecture, made possible through an endowment to Fairfield University by Larry Roberts and Suzanne Novik, honors the memory of their parents who shared a love of the visual arts (Bettie was an award-winning portraiture painter, Sam an accomplished nature photographer) and were supporters of Fairfield University's Bennett Center. I can think of no one better suited to give this lecture than Norman Gorbaty, whose strong sense of Jewish self-identity can be seen in each of the pieces included in what is the first comprehensive gallery exhibition of Norman's Judaic works.

As a modern Jewish historian and theologian, I am struck by the ways in which he uses shapes, images, color, and movement to successfully convey the multi-faceted nature of Judaism as both religion and way of life. There is an immediacy about Norman's work that deeply moves me, drawing us into specific moments in the history, literary narrative, holiday celebrations, and life cycle events of the Jewish people. Reflecting the words of the Passover *seder* that enjoin us to remember the Israelites' years of servitude "as if we [ourselves] were slaves in the land of Egypt," Norman's uses art as remembrance. Through works that are astonishing in size, scope, and diversity of artistic expression, he makes us feel not just as though we *were* there, but as if we *are* there: underneath a *chuppah* (bridal canopy) in the *shul* (synagogue) in the Brooklyn neighborhood of his youth; dancing with a Torah on *Simchat Torah*, wrestling with the angel along with the biblical Jacob; walking with the Jewish orphans of the Warsaw ghetto as they were sent to their death.

The enormous wooden bas reliefs with which the Walsh Gallery exhibition opens, literally invite us into the biblical story of creation. Wide-eyed, the animals of the garden of Eden directly face us as we, like them, harmoniously stand next to the naked Adam and Eve, experiencing life in the idyllic garden. As both viewer and participant, we awake as Adam awakes, like Eve, we struggle with the serpent, and as Adam and Eve slowly walk out of the garden, their heads bowed, ashamed of their act of disobedience, our eyes are drawn to them, and we feel ourselves leaving the garden as well, into a world that is infinitely more complex and demanding.

As Norman Gorbaty's sculptures, paintings, and works on paper show, the world into which we are born is one in which life is alternately cherished and destroyed. It includes moments of joy, sadness, connection, loneliness, illumination, and horror. Norman's initial vision of life after Eden is universal. The birth of Cain, "the first murderer," signals the fact that our world is fraught with problems that human beings as a whole have created and to which we must reply as "***Godlike...caretakers.***" Yet as the works of art following the birth of Cain suggest, to Gorbaty, how we actually see the world, and whether or how we resolve to change it, is often rooted in the particular context of our lives. For Norman himself, that context is clearly Jewish. The son of Eastern European immigrants, he grew up with a strong sense of *Yiddishkeit* (Jewishness): speaking Yiddish in the home, celebrating Jewish holidays, living in a Jewish neighborhood in Brooklyn, and reading, or having read to him, works of Jewish literature. He listened to his mother's stories of the life she'd left behind and of her relatives who remained in Europe, including her parents, who along with other members of her family, perished during the holocaust. From his father, he learned that to be a Jew means to care for other human beings and to make the world more just. "From my mother," Norman told me, "I learned about the beauty of Judaism; from my father, I learned what it means to live as a Jew." From both of them, it seems, he came to identify strongly with the Jewish people, viewing Jewish history, not as a series of linear, external events, but rather as that which continues to take place within him. "I didn't ask to be a Jew," Norman has told me, "but it's who I am."

Thus, the human "problems" that Norman remembers through this exhibit are those that have beset the Jewish people. They include the massacre of Jews during the First Crusade, the anti-semitic pogroms of late 19th and 20th century Europe, trains that sent Jews in Nazi-occupied Europe to the death camps, and the refusal of the British and the Turks to give refuge to the hundreds of Romanian Jews who consequently died at sea in the dilapidated ship, the Struma. Similarly, the responses to such problems are Jewish ones, reflecting both historical reality and Jewish hopes and values. The Jewish orphans of Warsaw are not depicted as victims of the holocaust, but as those who, along with their teacher and mentor, Janusz Korzcak, silently and courageously marched to their death. The sculpture memorializing those who died aboard the Struma hoping to find refuge in Palestine, recalls the Jewish dream of the return to Zion, while the woman in the center of the bas-relief, holding up a baby in her out-stretched arms in an attempt to save him, is a reminder of the value of saving human life. Finally, giving visual expression to the rabbinic teaching not to despair of the world, the scenes of trains are not dark and riddled with shadow but strikingly infused with color and light.

The beauty of Judaism as a religion is lovingly conjured up in many of Gorbaty's works. Though Norman's own sense of Jewish self-identity is not expressed through regular synagogue attendance, his minimalist sculpture of a *bimah* (the stage from which prayer services are conducted) and pastels and charcoal drawings of Torah scrolls, synagogue menorahs (7 branched candelabrums), and *tallitot* (prayer shawls) bring us into the life of the synagogue. The angle from which the bride and groom of his "Marriage in the Synagogue" are viewed places us on the ground floor of the sanctuary, in the pews at the wedding. Similarly in "*kapporos*" (a ritual performed before Yom Kippur, practiced by few Jews today, in which a chicken takes on the community's sins), we imagine our face superimposed on the faceless boy of the drawing. Each of us, in other words, is present at a ritual which in all likelihood we have never witnessed.

In his book *Zakhor* (Hebrew for the imperative "remember"), historian Yosef Yerushalmi astutely notes that the nature of Jewish memory has never been dispassionate recollection but rather evocation, identification, and re-actualization. One finds all of these qualities in the Jewish art of Norman Gorbaty. Jewish identity is enriched, strengthened, and preserved through memory. Retelling, and as Gorbaty's works so powerfully remind us, reimaging and re-experiencing the past connect us to rich and valuable resources of comprehension and meaning.

Torah
26" x 40"
Pastel
1999

Norman Gorbaty: Wrestling With Angels – Real Or Imagined?

by Philip Eliasoph, Ph.D.

Philip Eliasoph, Ph.D. is Professor of Art History in the Department of Visual & Performing Arts. His career began studying non-objective art focusing on Kandinsky's theories and the evolution of modernist painting. He has become an expert on American social realist and academic painting, authoring books, curating exhibits, and writing articles about Paul Cadmus, Robert Vickrey, Robert Cottingham, and Colleen Browning, especially those working in the traditional Renaissance based, egg yolk tempera method. Last summer he was invited to lecture at the Pollock-Krasner House & Studio re-considering the tensions dividing the abstract and realist art camps.

Norman Gorbaty's "Torah" [pastel on paper, 1999] is a whirling, Cubo-Futurist meditation sanctifying the sacred scroll. Ark, silver bells, huddled worshippers are tightly bound together declaring "*Shema Y'Israel...*" — "Hear oh Israel... the Lord is One!"

Within its blinding vortex, it captures everything a Jew could hope to understand in its illumination. And yet, the smudged colors and evaporating lines of barely discernible *tallitot* and silver tower crowns are threaded together out of fragmented, minimally indicated strokes.

It's as if nothingness is transformed into something. Pictures are supposed to represent something else. But pictures are merely human fabrications made from clay, paint or chalk. Images are fictitious and should not be trusted or worshipped. Idolatry was deposed for its lies. Jews are taught that God is truth.

So in deference to the Tablets of the Law placed into the obedient hands of Moses some thirty-three centuries ago, those pictures became very problematic. The Decalogue's Second Commandment prohibited any "graven images."

This "chosen" bronze age tribe was directed to forgo any enfleshment of Yahweh. Other tribes had so much more to see and enjoy. Jews had to suffer. Ram headed statuettes in Sumeria, buxom fertility goddesses in the Aegean islands, or cosmic deities with the sleek bodies of muscular lions in Egypt, all caused some real '*tsores*' in terms of Jewish image-making.

Curator Norman Kleeblatt of the Jewish Museum lets us escape out the other hatch as Jewish artists since antiquity seem to be "inhabiting a different cultural space." On *Shabbos* morning, the rabbi holds up the ancient scrolls on the *bimah* and beseeches us: "Behold!"

Gorbaty places this before our eyes to wonder: "Behold — this might just be an illusion!" Using Judaism's most central object of worship and wisdom, he almost taunts us: "How can Jewish identity be expressed — if at all?"

Tracing our steps backwards into the early decades of the 20th century, opens a window into some of "Torah's" pictorial secrets. Gorbaty's drawing evokes the non-Euclidean space of the Picasso-Braque 'roped together mountain climbing team' in their ascent into the netherworld. A continuous flow of staccato photographic frames were built in Duchamp's staircase.

The slanting racing car effect of Gino Severini and kinetic pace of speeding trains in Boccioni and Marinetti are palpable. Some spatial vorticism of El Lissitzsky or Natalie Goncharova adds a dizzying, Suprematist accent. And let's not overlook the jazzy rhythms of Stuart Davis, or Stanton MacDonald-Wright. "Torah" is a sturdy lesson in avant-gardist image-making.

There is in fact so little to actually see — we are confronted with a profound conflict. Thinking about Norman Gorbaty's art in the context of his Jewish identity is both essential and useless. "In every cell of my body I am a Jew," he admits. Then, with a sigh as if casting off the weight of Job he exhales: "honestly, I don't really understand the where, when, or how this impacts my art. It's all a mystery. But I am absolutely certain its in the DNA of every brushstroke and scrap of wood which peels off of my chisel. Don't ask me why — it just happens."

I had learned a little about Norman reviewing articles in glossy magazines, flipping through a lavishly illustrated book about his multi-faceted career, and sensing the man's indefatigable energies. From a distance, through a series of impressive publications, I had only an incomplete snapshot of his creative output. But it was not until we finally sat down for a quiet morning conversation did I come to appreciate his arsenal of talents. Gorbaty is unequivocally a deeply experienced and unimaginably gifted artist-creator-thinker.

One might envision Norman as a living Al Hirschfeld caricature. His pixie-like '*ponem*' is etched with creviced life-lines. The man's entire bearing is all larger than the sum of its parts. His face is Rembrandt-esque with its expressively searching, soulful eyes. With his Eastern Parkway inflection, he speaks in sharp little jabs. His language bristles like a flurry of quick punches from the gloves of young Cassius Clay.

Norman's firm opinions form phrases which 'sting like a bee.' He's quick to interrupt, counter, and jump-in. You can't get a word in edgewise. Conversing with Norman is exhausting and exhilarating. Inevitably, one realizes you've lost any point of contention before you could even begin. As he shrugs and gesticulates you realize — why argue? Just accept it: he's right. Always.

It did not escape me during our '*kibitsing*' session this vintaged gentleman could have been easily been any one of my uncles who were honored at my Bar Mitzvah to say the *motzi* prayer. 'Get this over with, slice the *challah*, honor its traditions, but let the party begin,' was their attitude. Norman also admits. "I was never a religious man — but I know I am a Jew."

There's little doubt in his presence about his authenticity as a living treasure. Having this exhibition opportunity for Fairfield University to review his prolific contributions — as an artist who "just so happens to be Jewish" — and as an under-appreciated artistic voice in our midst — is surely a celebratory milestone.

Norman exudes a Picasso-like verve for eternal youthfulness. He carries himself with a 'Zorba-esque' vitality for life. Chronological age must only be a illusory notion in his psyche. He drinks from the most potent elixir of youth: his art. But in more subtle and revealing ways, I believe Norman's anguished expression traces back to Sholem Aleichem's over-burdened Tevye. He reminds us of that archetype of the quintessentially good, decent, hard-working, devoted family patriarchal provider. Tevye always wished he could abandon his duties milking cows to sit in '*shul*' all day and become a 'learned man.'

As Jewish history is cyclical and simultaneously immediate — we are eternally present at the foot of Mount Sinai as we open the Haggadah each Passover — Norman conveys an awareness of the weight of our peoplehood. Family duties and responsibilities in czarist Anatevka, were the same obligations Norman felt in Great Neck and the New York art world. I know instinctively that Norman would have liked to just paint and sculpt all day in his art studio.

But there were bills to pay, children to provide for, and the vicissitudes of being successful in upscale Lake Success. There are diversions on the obstacle course. Keeping up with the status minded Jacokowitz's and Judstein's on Meadow Woods Road, demanded working hard, and churning out those massively profitable marketing campaigns and commercial designs. Life was filled with gratification. But he kept itching to return to his studio.

His rich visual ideas were splashed across the pages of **Time**, **Fortune**, and **U.S. News & World Report**, or in the credit scroll for three of Woody Allen's films. Fame, professional achievement, and a mountain of professional career rewards. Questioning God's ambiguous plan for his art career, he might have looked up to the Almighty to ask: "If I were a wealthy man?"

Norman was rewarded for his creative genius in taking the motivational research of Vance Packard's "The Hidden Persuaders" [1957] by translating American's feelings into consumer purchasing power. But at the same time, he knew he was competing on the rat-race treadmill from "What Makes Sammy Run?" Bud Shulberg's novel was published in 1941. But it was the Philco Television Theatre production on 1949 which gained public awareness. It's message for those on the career escalator: "death is the only finish line."

Norman was cut out of the same mold as many of the fathers of my school buddies in Great Neck. When one friend's father drove us *schmendricks* to a Bar Mitzvah at an elite country club [Jews preferred British sounding names with references to oaks, foxes, hunt, ivy, etc.] in a huge white Lincoln Continental, the 'sweet taste of success' was an intoxicant. I felt I was stepping in JFK's doomed Dallas vehicle – as we opened the opposing swing doors and stepped into this 5,200 pound machine. The 1964 ad campaign offered its owners a seductive lure with its 123" wheel base, V-8 "enlarged for added power."

The bar mitzvah itself was on a scale of the Corleone wedding scene on Lake Tahoe from 'The Godfather.' A generation after European Jewry had perished in the ovens, they were inventing the Big Ideas in marketing, advertising, and media that the Madison Avenue agencies executed to make Pepsi and Pepto-Bismol into global brands at the very summit of America's empire.

Over the years I have had the privilege of interviewing and writing essays about other noteworthy artists of Norman's caliber. They too were conflicted in finding themselves in a struggle between their fine art studio passions versus their 'bread-and-butter-pay-the-mortgage-and-kids-tuition-bills' careers as artistic dynamos serving the seductive world of the 'Mad Men.' Who wants to be a 'starving artist' when your expense account allows lunches at the Four Seasons?

During those 'go-go' years, at the peak of Henry Luce's imperial 'American Century,' an unquenchable thirst for consumer products transformed the lives of these incredibly talented artists into 'work for hire' designers. If I am not wrong, Michelangelo also painted a ceiling as a commission, and Bernini installed a few fountains around the piazzas of Rome at the behest of his noble patrons.

At the same time, I had the uncanny vision of Norman as a deeply intellectual version of Milton Berle, Sid Caesar, or Alan King. What made them so different from the non-Jewish comedians, why were they so inscrutable with their self-deprecating jokes and 'outsider looking in' humor while we watched Ed Sullivan on the old black and white Zenith box in our family room? Ask Norman.

I began to wish we had the time to sit at Katz's Deli on Houston Street. I wanted to listen more to Norman's anecdotes, and pick at my pastrami and sour pickles, to learn about his early years in the New York art world. Like that misty lens in Irving Howe's "World of Our Fathers," this now lost 'golden' era in the 1950s-60s was a time when the discourse about art was serious within a 'no-nonsense' frame.

Jewish giants — Mark Rothko, Louise Nevelson, Adolph Gottlieb, Helen Frankenthaler, Barnett Newman — walked the earth. These secular Jews contributed to and helped to invent [along with their non-Jewish colleagues, Pollock, Gorky, Hofmann, de Kooning, Motherwell, Still, etc.] a new terrain — the uniquely American and "Made in Manhattan" style of Abstract Expressionism. They aspired to and eventually changed the very nature of art history — there was no turning back.

Many art historians and critics came to understand how the New York School transformed modern art. Artists of Gorbaty's generation considered abstraction as a virtual "religion for atheists." Rothko actually quipped that the people who "weep before my paintings are having the same religious experience I felt when painting them."

The 2010 TONY-Award winning Broadway drama, "Red" is an on-stage re-creation of Rothko's painting liturgy. Like a muted clergyman, he is dwarfed by towering color-field canvases — consumed by orange-reds-maroons — like Moses agape before the Burning Bush. Awe.

The funny thing — so Jewishly ironic — is that none of the Jewish modernists wanted to be known or have their works contextualized as being "Jewish." No wonder this confused consciousness shaped a polemical 1996 exhibition at the Jewish Museum of New York. "Too Jewish: Challenging Jewish Identities," by exploiting and exploding a number of visual tropes and stereotypes.

It's difficult to re-create today the driving forces which shaped the intelligentsia of the art scene just after Gorbaty completed his M.F.A at Yale in 1955. It was a curious hybrid with these elements:

1] Art - mainly abstraction, or at least post-European with its roots in Cubism, Futurism, Expressionism, and Surrealism. The Museum of Modern Art made 'good design' [Eames chairs, Ekco flatware, Watrous lamps, Earl Tupper plastics] into a way of life.

2] Politics - RedScare - with old-style Stalinists who closed their eyes to Stalin's capitulation to Nazism in signing the Molotov-Ribbentrop nonaggression pact with Hitler in 1939 locked in debate with the John Birch Society predicting that subversive Bolsheviks were fluoridating public water systems and stealing our hydrogen bomb secrets. Left leaning Jewish socialists were constantly compromised in loyalties to core Norman Rockwell-esque American freedoms vs. social justice issues necessitating vigorous dissent. The Rosenbergs betrayal had created a '*shanda*' while major legal and financial support for fighting Jim Crow laws in the South was coming from Jewish organizations, rabbis, and civil rights advocates.

3] American global supremacy — infused with the post-war 'can-do' optimism, the construction of vast suburban tracts, inter-state highways, and commercialized galaxy of products promoted by television's omni-presence in millions of homes. General Motors and General Mills were the envy of the world while products invaded living rooms during commercial breaks for "I Love Lucy" to "The Honeymooners."

He was trained and educated at Smith, Amherst, and Yale probably believing he was destined to become a fine artist. But like the Israelites 40 years wanderings through the Sinai's wilderness, Norman's detour from his fine art studio sent him off on a 60 year journey. Along the way, he achieved international distinctions as one of the leading graphic designers of our age. His resume as a brilliantly innovative commercial artist and graphic designer is chock full of coveted medals, professional awards, and Oscar-like golden calves attesting to his creative genius.

Wrestling like his memorable bas-relief bronze — "Peniel", 1987, of Jacob's body twisted into a knot with an angelic form, Norman's position as a Jewish artist is equally entwined. Whether he accepts or rejects this destiny — he is inevitably inscribed in the unwrapping *megillah* of so-called 'Jewish art.'

Every inspiring sermon I have ever heard greeting the New Year on Rosh Hashanah morning comes from the pulpit with this indispensible central motif: 'the Quote'. This was usually an obscure talmudic or scriptural reference which connects the wisdom of the ages with the congregants of today.

Rabbis must search for 'the Quote' as popular novelists must ponder the first sentence of their next best-seller. It has to have multiple layers of deeply connected, mind-numbing symbolism. The concept is to inspired those in the present with the spiritual conflicts and ethical crises of the past.

As a schoolboy, I can still remember how our revered Oxford-educated rabbi would take a dramatic pause — and somehow I could anticipate the next sentence — it was then completed with a polished jewel from the lips of Rabbi Hillel, Rabbi Akiba, the Rambam — Maimonides, or the Baal Shem Tov. More modern flourishes came in quotes from Max Jacob, Chaim Potok, or Issac Bashevich Singer. Our 'old school rebbe' would never touch Saul Bellow, Norman Mailer, or Philip Roth. They were just far too assimilated or 'edgy.'

So here is my favorite source of Jewish artistic '*seykhl*'. It came out of the mind of the art sage Harold Rosenberg [1906-1978]. He was the ideologically bent, cultural connoisseur of leftist 'art has sociological purposes' offering his genius in the pages of the **ARTnews**, **Partisan Review** and most regularly, **The New Yorker**. His seminal 1952 read on the New York school gave birth to the movement/verb/phrase: "Action Painting." Rosenberg was unassailable.

The year is 1966. Imagine an upscale, highly educated audience of Manhattan's 'smart set' culturati streaming into the newly opened temple for Jewish art [paradoxically] at Fifth Avenue and 92nd St. The former mansion of Felix and Frieda Shiff Warburg, was transformed into the Jewish Museum. Its rather unfocused mission was to present and preserve Jewish identity in the visual arts. The program began as Rosenberg arrived at the podium followed by a hushed silence. His opening salvo pretty much said it all:

"First, they build a Jewish museum; then they ask, 'Is there a Jewish art?" Jews!" The author of the modern art criticism bible, "**The De-Definition of Art**" then disassembled the anxious crowd even further. "The gentile answer is, 'Yes, there is a Jewish art, and no there is no Jewish art.'" He continued: "But the Jewish answer is, 'What do you mean by Jewish art?'"

In these artworks which were born out of a marvelously endowed artistic consciousness, it seems pointless to label, categorize, or minimize his clearly realized vision.

If art is a tongue spoken by all who can see, feel, and love — he has transcended any of the narrowing limitations of his age. The most validating evidence of Norman Gorbaty's "Jewishness" is manifested in the eloquent mysteries within these paintings, drawings, and sculptures. Gorbaty also chants a resoundingly heard universal prayer: "***L'Chaim***" — To Life!

In 1954 Norman Gorbaty was a promising young artist whose work was included in a modest show of Young American Printmakers at New York's Museum of Modern Art. At Amherst he earned the Heisey Award for design in glass from Steuben and was honored with a scholarship to attend the inaugural session of the newly formed Yale Norfolk Summers Arts School. Upon graduating he received a Simpson fellowship from Amherst and a teaching fellowship from Yale where he enrolled to pursue his MFA. While at Yale, Gorbaty found himself in a rich artistic environment influenced by teachers that included Joseph Albers, Alexi Brodovitch, Leo Leonni, Herbert Matter, Bernard Chaet, Gabor Peterdi and Louis Kahn, as well as students that included Richard Anuszkiewicz, Neil Welliver, William Bailey, Arnie Bittleman and Jay Maisel. During this time at Yale, Gorbaty won the Summer Painting Prize from Joseph Albers and had his prints regularly shown in the prestigious Brooklyn Museum Printmaking Annual. His master's thesis Print Making with a Spoon was published by Reinhold and incorporated in almost its entirety in Gabor Peterdi's authoritative volume Printmaking Methods Old and New. 1954 was also the year that Gorbaty proposed to Joy Marks. They married in 1956 when practical considerations and pressures led him from a career in fine art towards one in graphic design. He honed his skills as a graphic artist working at Benton and Bowles Advertising as the Vice President Art Group Supervisor where he directed the product launch of many now familiar brands including the IBM Selective Typewriter, Pampers and Crest Toothpaste. During this time he was invited to be the Adjunct Profressor of Advanced Graphic Design at Cooper Union where he taught for almost a decade. Upon leaving Benton and Bowles, Gorbaty opened his own graphic design studio in 1968. His work included credits for major motion pictures, museum posters, magazine covers for Time and US News & World Report, and illustrations for numerous children's books. Gorbaty has received recognition and awards for his work and has been asked to lecture at a host of schools including Yale, Carnegie-Mellon, Minneapolis School of Art and the Kansas City School of Art.

Throughout his fifty years as a graphic artist Gorbaty continued to produce fine art amassing a large body of work that includes sculpture, paintings and works on paper. With the passing of Joy, his "Old Beauty" in 2003, Gorbaty no longer had his audience-of-one with whom to share his art. Having accomplished his goal of providing Joy and their two children with stability and comfort he again turned his entire focus back to fine art.

I have always been a doer of images. Anything that strikes my fancy is ready for the doing: birth, death, building, destruction, beauty, ugliness — the wonder of it — the mystery of it all — of line, shape, color, space, and movement. The mystery is in the doing.

In all my doing, Jewish themes keep emerging. Not unusual in that I am a Jew. These images speak to the suffering of my people, and the contributions they have made to mankind. I make visual statements to save from anonymity those who have suffered for being Jews throughout history: to never forget the road we Jews are traveling. For as a Jew, I am doing history. The future, the present, and the past meld into one along this road. We do Judaism. I am as much in the past of my people as I am into today or the future. I recall the words of a friend Arbit Blatas, who did the extraordinary 7 bas-relief tablets commemorating the Holocaust now hanging in the Venice Ghetto:

"I know only that I must do them — out of my people's past, in memory of my mother and father, in memory of six million, in memory of the hundreds of millions of Jews killed through the ages."

We owe it to those, who know nothing of our road that they be taught never to forget. Along with our sufferings as "Jobs" of history, we have made, beyond our numbers, great impact on what we call civilization.

And so, using the forms, shapes and symbols of Judaism, I honor my people.

CREATION SERIES

Where are we? Where do we come from? Where are we going? The eternal questions we ask ourselves. The passage of "from" to "to." From innocence to "reality." Creation – it's about breaking the rules and finding oneself in a different world – outside comfortable known borders. A world for which we are now responsible. Where we become the caretakers.

The Animals
48" x 72"
Pine
1973

Creation of Adam
48" x 72"
Pine
1975

Creation of Eve

48" x 72"

Pine

1977

Eden
48" x 72"
Pine
1980

The Temptation
48" x 72"
Pine
1981

Expulsion
48" x 72"
Pine
1998

The "birth" of the first murderer. In a world, not Eden, where we are destined to live and make reply to problems we create. Where we are destined to be Godlike as care-takers of the world.

Birth of Cain
24" x 24"
Basswood
1984

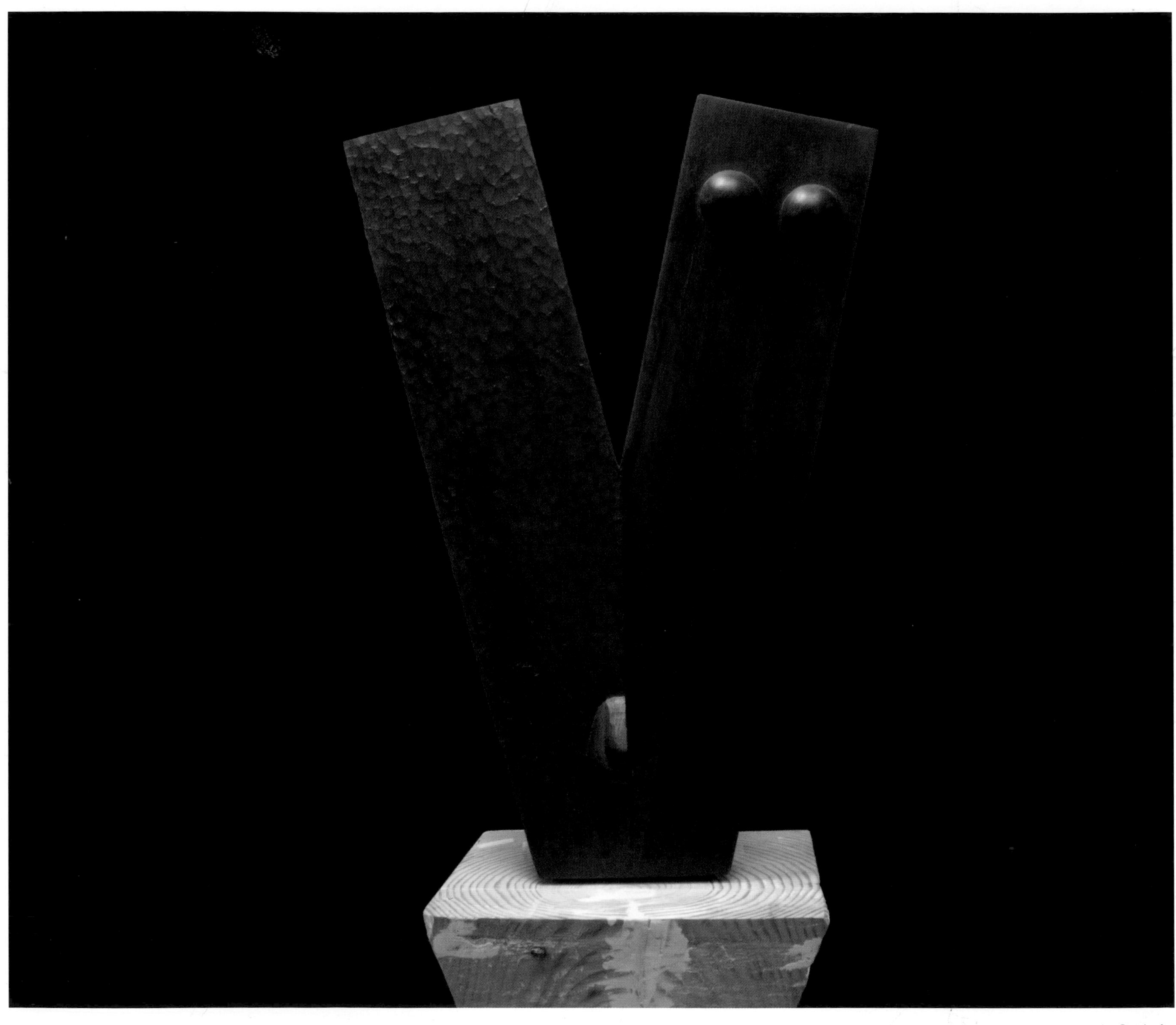

Eve from Adam
22 3/4" x 15 3/4" x 5"
Fir
2007

Bimah
7" x 8" x 8"
Bronze
1962

Overleaf:
Bimah
40" x 78"
Pastel
2004

Shabbat Wedding
40" x 42"
Pastel
2000

Torah
26" x 40"
Pastel
1999

Shabbat Menorah
26" x 40"
Charcoal
1999

Following Page:
Shabbat
40" x 78"
Pastel
2006

Menorah – Shul

40" x 26"

Pastel

2004

Shabbat
Candle sticks
40" x 26"
Pastel
2002

Marriage in the Synagogue
40" x 78"
Pastel
1999

Jewish Wedding
40" x 78"
Pastel
1998

Groom with Bride
40" x 26"
Pastel
2000

Jewish Bride
26" x 20"
Charcoal
2007

Jacob spent the night alone on the far side of the Jabbok River, and there he wrestled with an unknown presence, a man, an angel, God, until break of day. In the course of the wrestling as day approached, the man said, 'Let me go, for the day is breaking', and Jacob replied, 'I will not let you go unless you bless me'. The man asks Jacob's name, and when he is told, says that from now on your name is Israel, 'for you have striven with God and man and have prevailed'. In return, Jacob asks him his name, but is not told. The man simply blesses him, and Jacob calls the place where this happens 'Peniel', because there he saw God 'face to face'.

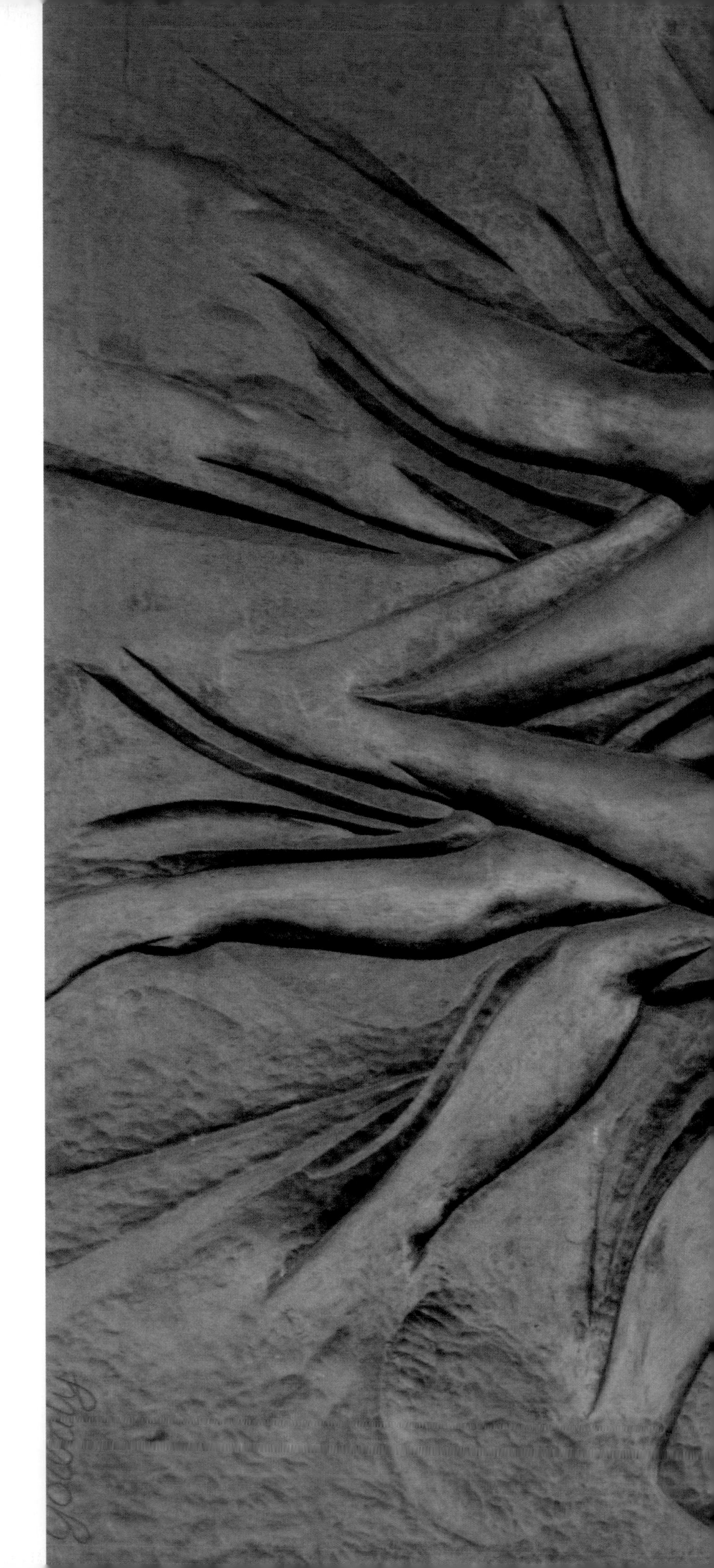

Peniel
72" x 96"
Bronze
1987

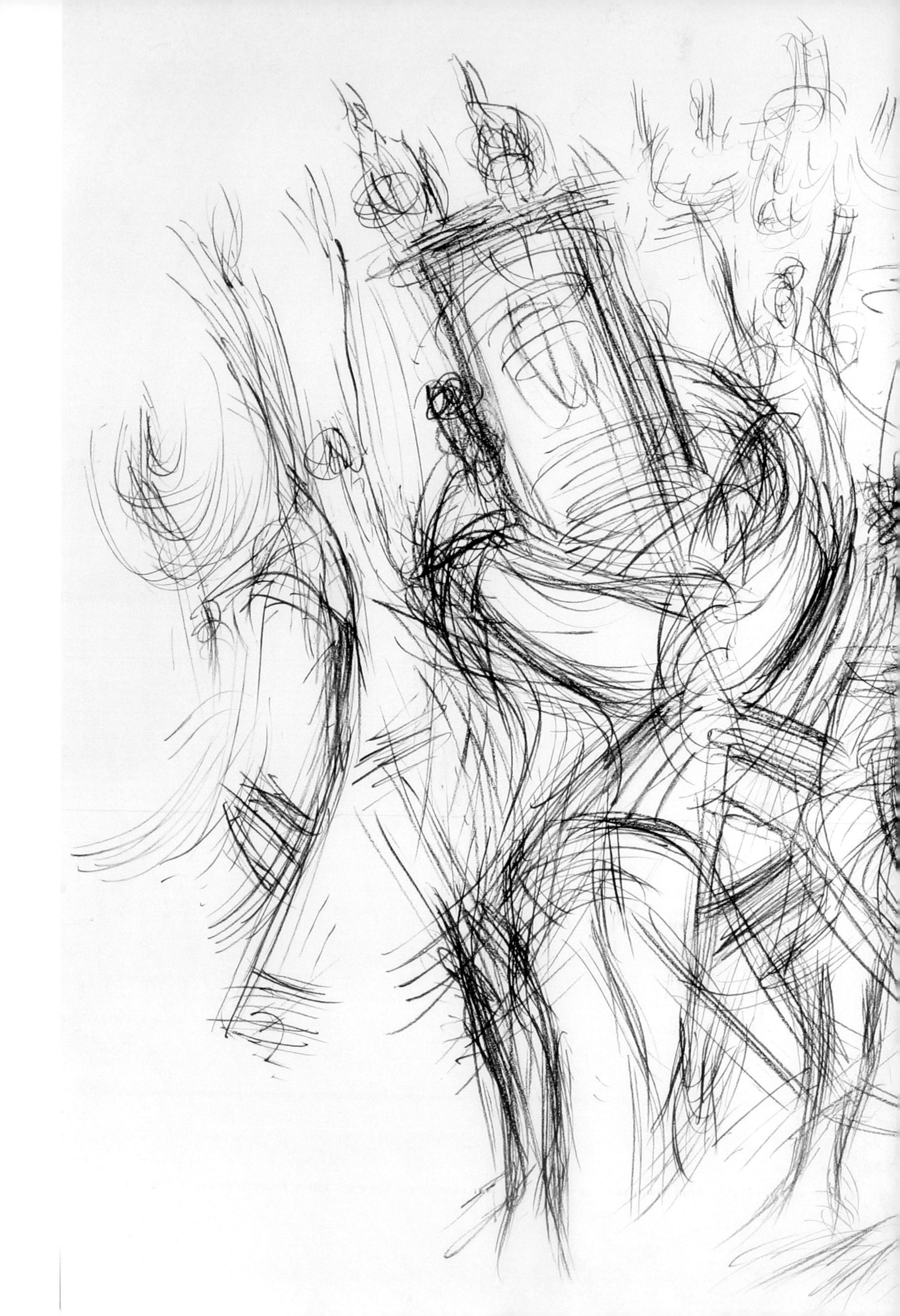

Simchas Torah
26" x 40"
Charcoal
2001

Following Page:
Simchas Torah
40" x 78"
Pastel
2001

Adoration of the Moon
40" x 26"
Charcoal
2008

Shofar
Rosh Hashanah
40" x 26"
Charcoal
2008

Kapporos
40" x 26"
Charcoal
2005

For Love of
Torah
40" x 26"
Charcoal
2009

Shtettel
15 3/4" x 20 3/4"
Pen & Brown Ink
1982

Pogrom No.2
Pencil
1988

Pogrom
5 1/2" x 7 1/2"
Pen & Ink
1978

The Dead I

40" x 26"

Charcoal Pencil

2010

The Dead II
40" x 26"
Charcoal Pencil
2010

STRUMA

December 12, 1942
The decrepit, unseaworthy ship, Struma set sail from Romania with 769 Jews seeking passage to Palestine to escape the danger of impending Nazi occupation. Three days, after much delay, due to engine failure, the severely overcrowded ship with minimal facilities was towed into Istanbul.

The British government at the time did not want Jews to emigrate to Palestine. The Turkish government influenced by the British and for its own reasons refused to land the ships passengers. A few passengers with expired Palestinian visas and a pregnant woman were allowed to disembark. The rest remained overcrowded aboard the ship for two months with little food, and no toilet facilities. Finally the ship with no functioning engine was towed out to sea by the Turkish government where it drifted helplessly. It floundered and is said to have been sunk inadvertently by a Russian submarine on February 24, 1942. All 763 passengers perished except for one David Stoliar, while clinging to wreckage, was found and rescued by a row boat sent out by a watchtower along the Turkish coast.

Struma
60" x 84"
Walnut
1984

Kielce Pogrom
(Work in progress)
60" x 84"
Ebonized Walnut
2010

KIELCE POGROM

Occured on July 4, 1946, one year *after* the end of World War II and the Holocaust. 42 Jews were murdered, among them women and children. Nine were shot dead, two were killed with bayonets, the rest were beaten or stoned to death.

The Catholic church's position on the pogrom as expressed by various priests, bishops and cardinals was that the Jews had brought it on themselves.

One year after the end of World War II and the Holocaust.

IN MEMORIAM

The first crusade (1095 AD) is generally presented as a holy war against a Moslem threat to Christendom. Little mention is made of the destruction of Jewish communities throughout Europe, especially along the Rhine, where more than 14,000 Jews were killed by peasants and crusaders on their way to Jerusalem. The Jews in many instances showed a willingness to die for their faith, (Kiddach be-Shem), by suicide rather than convert to Christianity or to suffer the indignities imposed upon them by the Christian crusaders.

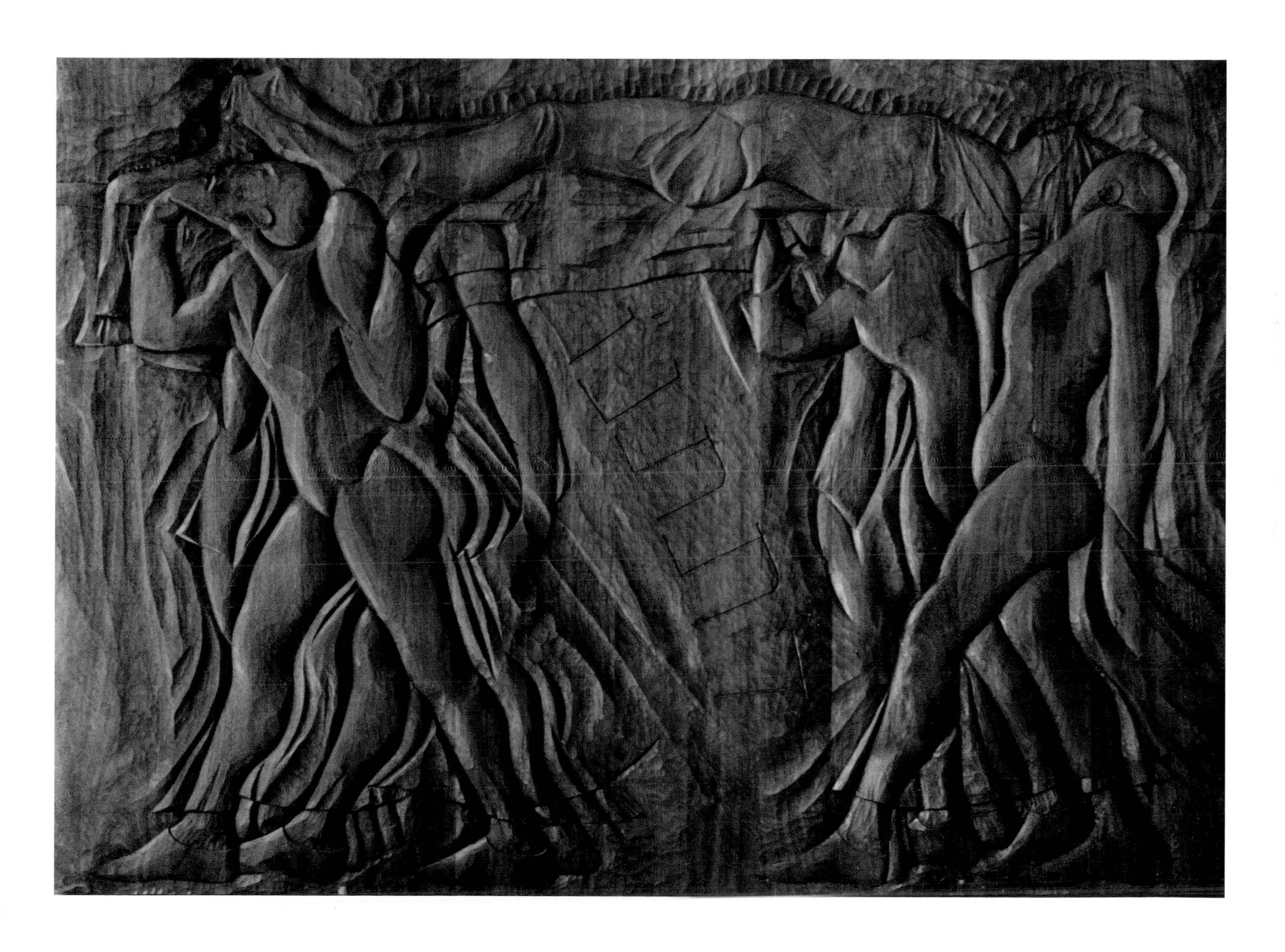

4856 (In memoriam)

60" x 84"

Walnut

1992

"The train...
the train,
it took
them to
the camps"

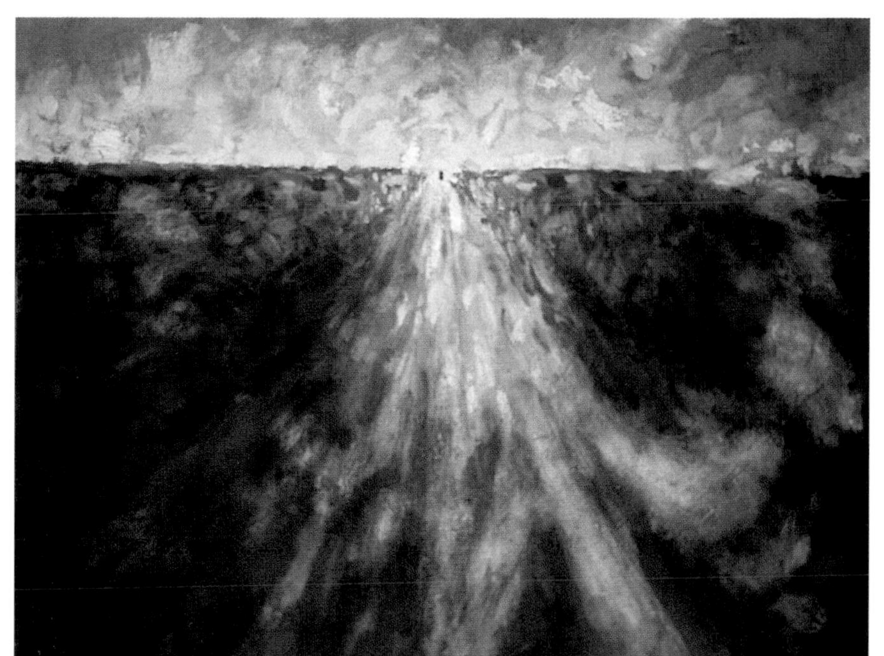

Train (series)
19 3/4" x 24"
Oil on Canvas
2005

"Our strongest bond with life is the child's open and radiant smile."

Janusz Korczak

Janusz Korczak was born in Warsaw Poland to an assimilated, socially concerned jewish family. Trained as a pediatrician he became famous as an author of children's books, newspaper and magazine articles and pedagogical books such as *How to Love a Child, When I am Small Again, A Child's Right to Respect*, in which he advanced his theories on teaching the whole child. In administrating a jewish orphanage, Dom Sierot in Warsaw he was able to put his progressive theories into practice. It was a place where children structured their own world and became expert in their own matters. He urged that the child be respected. Every child should be dealt with as an individual. He believed that every child is an individual whose inclinations, ambitions and conditions under which he or she is growing up requires understanding. Children differ but little from adults.

"Children are not future people, because they are people already. Children are people whose souls contain the seeds of all those thoughts and emotions that we possess. So as these seeds develop, their growth must be gently directed." — Janusz Korczak

The orphanage had its own internal court of honour, which had jurisdiction over both children and teachers; there were close relations between the staff and children. Every Sunday a general assembly was held. It was a country unto itself.

The orphanage was moved into the Ghetto when the Nazi's conquered Poland. Finally in August 5, 1942, the order was given for the entire body of the orphanage to report to the train station the next morning, Korczak was offered sanctuary but refused, insisting on staying with his children. That morning 192 children

Procession
Janusz Korczak Memorial
50 1/2" x 11" x 222"
Sculpture
Wood
2009

were dressed in their best clothes each carrying a blue knapsack with a favorite book, toy or musical instrument. An eyewitness described the procession of Korczak and his children through the ghetto.

"...A miracle occurred. Two hundred children did not cry out. Two hundred pure souls, condemned to death, did not weep. Not one of them ran away. None tried to hide. Like stricken swallows they clung to their teacher and mentor, to their father and brother, Janusz Korczak, so that he might protect and preserve them. Janusz Korczak was marching, his head bent forward holding the hand of a child, without a hat, a leather belt around his waist, and wearing high boots. A few nurses were followed by two hundred children, dressed in clean and meticulously cared for clothes, as they were being carried to the altar. (...) On all sides the children were surrounded by Germans, Ukrainians, and this time also Jewish policemen. They whipped and fired shots at them. The very stones of the street wept at the sight of the procession."

He boarded the trains with his children. They were never heard from again.

Following Page:
Procession
40" x 78"
Charcoal
2010

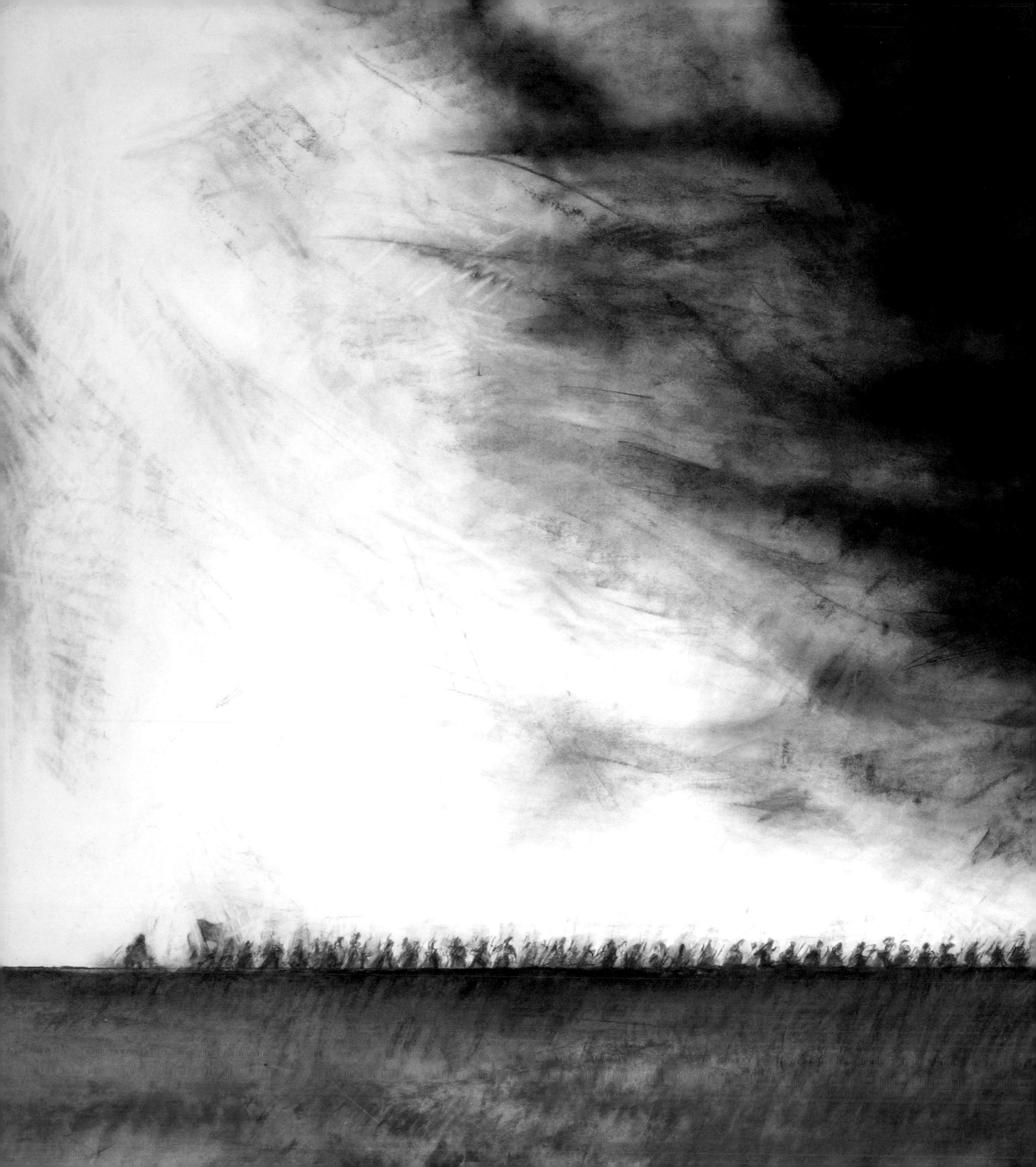

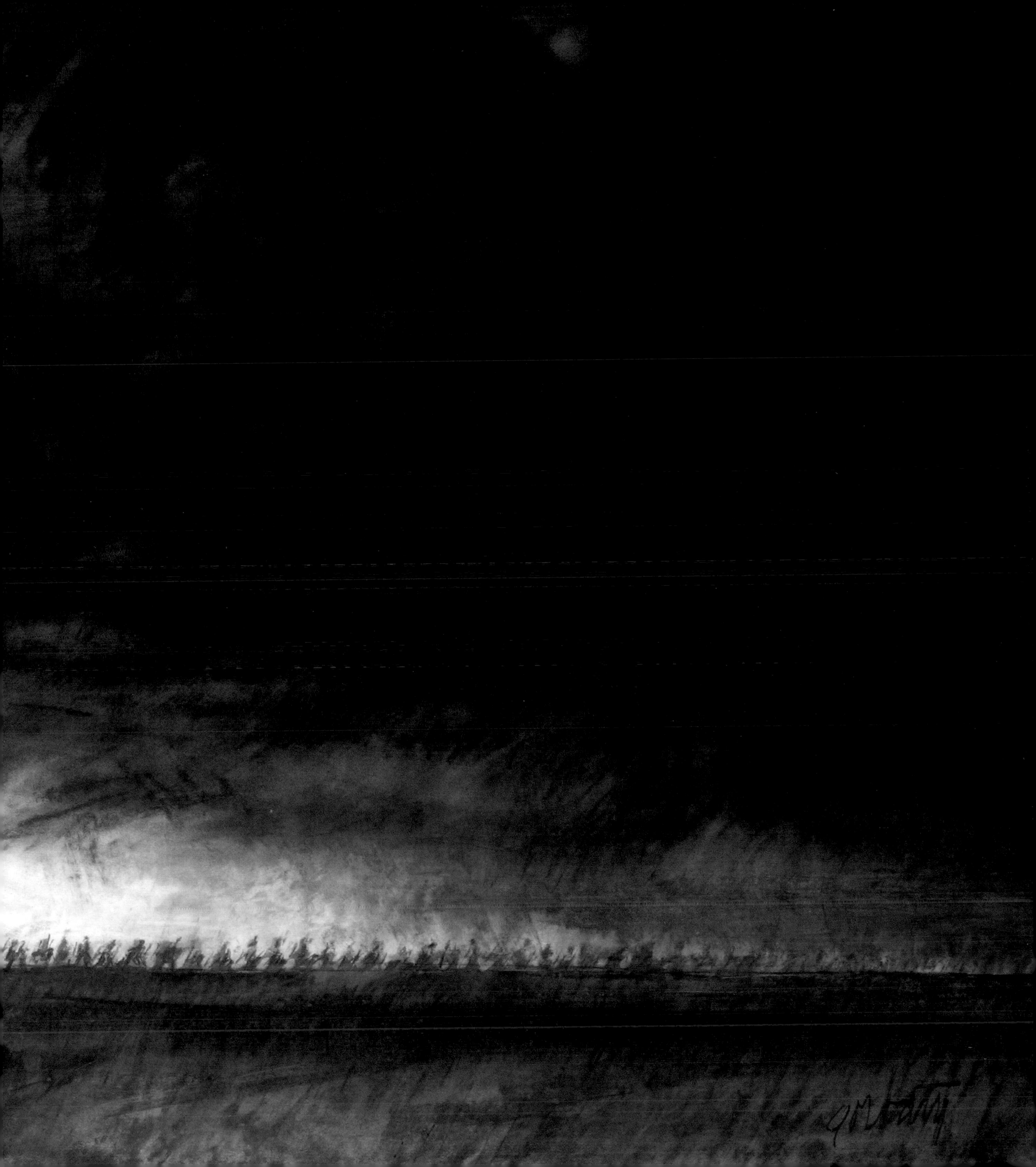

Talmud

17 1/2" x 24"

Casien Cut

1954

Pilpul
20" x 26"
Charcoal
2008

Shtender (series)
40" x 30"
Oil on Canvas
2003

Previous Page:

Shul

40" x 78"

Charcoal

1994

Shakina No.2

26" x 40"

Pastel

1998

Shakina No.1

26" x 40"

Pastel

1998

And

For

The

Children

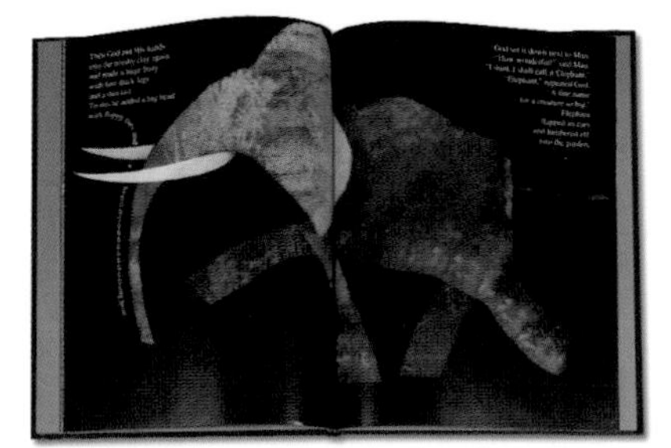

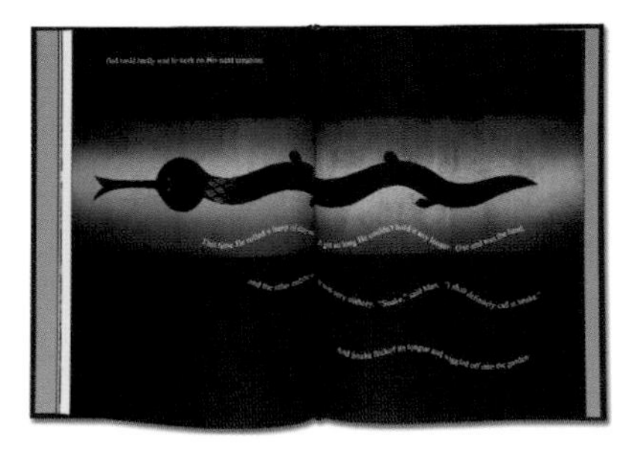

God's Gift
Publisher: Doubleday
Printing Ink, Roller, Stencil
1993

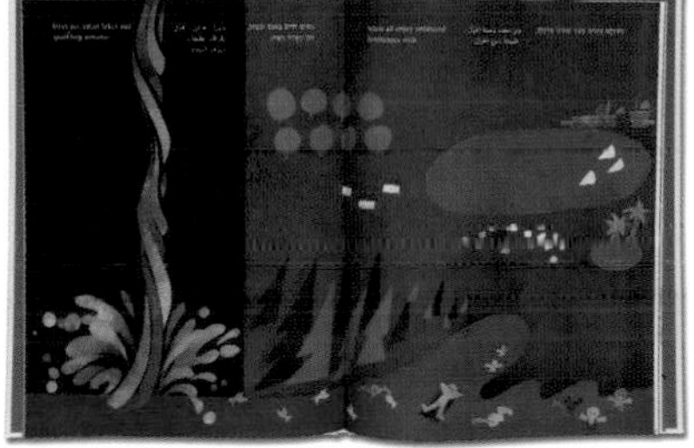

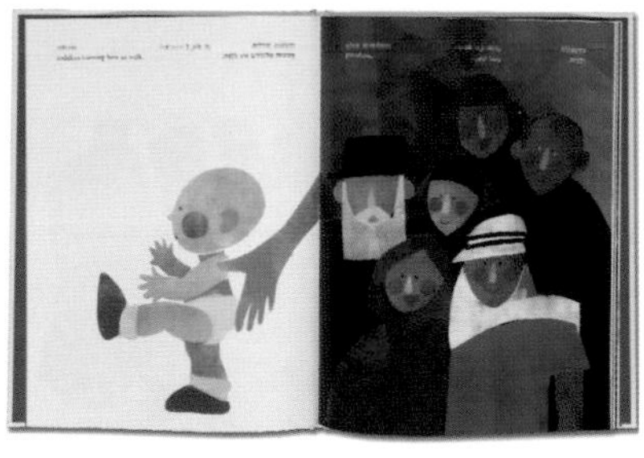

Shalom, Salaam, Peace
Publisher: CCAR
Printing Ink, Roller, Stencil
1999

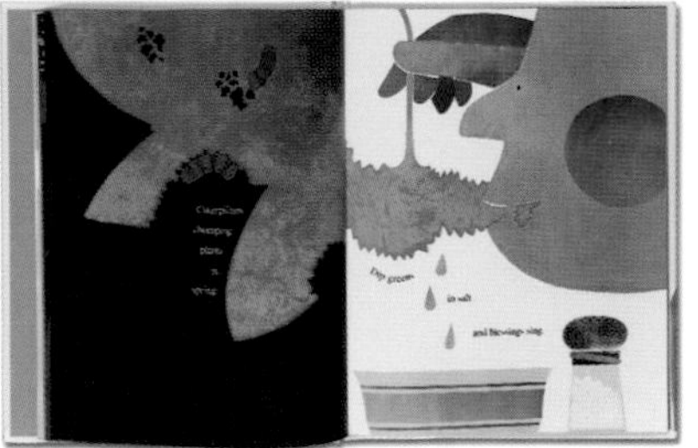

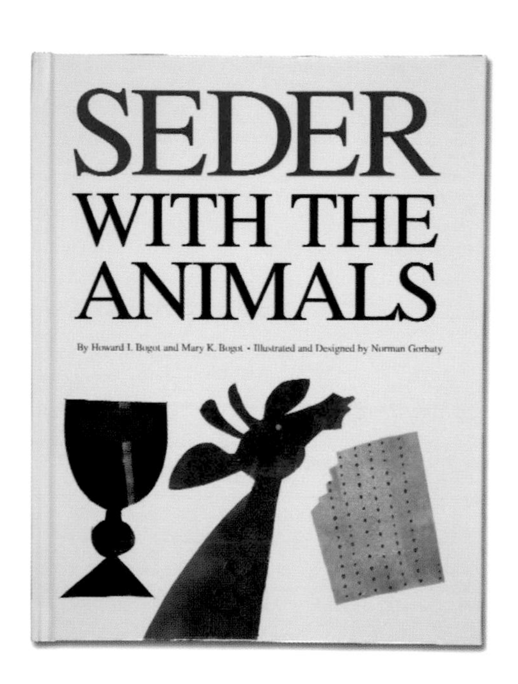

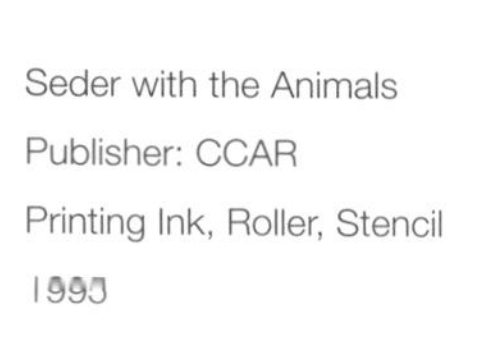

Seder with the Animals
Publisher: CCAR
Printing Ink, Roller, Stencil
1995

Thank You

This book represents the culmination of what began as a six month project and grew into a five year journey. There were many obstacles along the way that needed to be overcome. Our hope is, together with Works Of A Modern Master, this book will help Norman get the recognition and acknowledgement he deserves. We know how significant this journey was for Norman but it was deeply rewarding for us as well.

We'd like to thank the following people who were particularly helpful with respect to this project. Terry Birnbaum, Larry Bloom, Jill Deupi, Philip Eliasoph, Dan Hakim, Rabbi Yehoshua & Freida Hecht, Sylvia Herskowitz, Michelle LaRocca, Frances Iger-Laterman & Bernard Laterman, Steven Lichtenstein, Kevin Parks, Andrew Patapis, Meir Rhodes, Rabbi Levi & Chanie Stone: The Schneerson Center for Jewish Life, CT, Jon Stillman, Ellen Umansky, Reba Wulkan.

bg / skg

At Fairfield University, it was Diana Mille who first recognized the importance of Norman's Judaic work. Without her vision this exhibition would not have happened. For this we are grateful.

This all began with my love of my father's work and a passionate belief that the work needed to be shared with a broader audience. His Judaic work, specifically, was the key that opened the door to my own journey. What had begun as an exercise in organization and promotion evolved into one of spiritual revelation and self discovery. It was during our effort to expose my father's Judaic work that led me to Rabbi Levi Stone, a Chabad Lubavitcher Rabbi. Levi led me to Crown Heights, to Israel and to a greater understanding of Judaism and a deeper awareness of my own identity as a Jew. The journey with Levi, his family and friends has been deeply satisfying in ways beyond those I could have ever imagined. My life has changed forever.

What we did through this project was simply....put my father's work in a "pretty" package....to show it in a pleasant light.

The work is the work, it speaks for itself.

L'Chaim!

bg

Date of Birth

Born 1932
Brooklyn, NY

Education

1953-1955 **Yale University**
School of Art and Architecture
M.F.A.
Teaching Fellowship

1952 **Yale Norfolk Art School**
Adjunct Course work

1949-1953 **Amherst College**
B.A.
Magna Cum Laude, Phi Beta Kappa
Simpson Fellowship

1951-1953 **Smith College**
Adjunct Course work

Employment

1955-1956 **James Eng Associates**
Designer

1956-1958 **L.W. Frohlich**
Designer

1959-1968 **Benton & Bowles, Inc.**
Vice president, Art Group Supervisor

1968-Present **Norman Gorbaty Design, Inc.**
President – Designer

Instructor

1955-Summer **Yale Norfolk Art School**
Instructor

1961-1970 **Cooper Union School of Art**
Adjunct Professor
Advanced Graphic Design

1971 **Silvermine School of Art**
Instructor
Graphic Design

Visiting Lecturer

Yale University

Minneapolis School of Art

University of Winnipeg

University of Maine, Augusta

Carnegie-Mellon University

Kansas City School of Art

The Pennsylvania State University

Union College

Collections

Yale University Art Gallery
New Haven, CT

Baruch College
New York, NY

Glucksman Ireland House
New York University, New York, NY

Mead Art Museum
Amherst College, Amhest, MA

Print Research Foundation
Stamford, CT

The Eric Carle Museum of Picture Book Art
Amherst, MA

National Portrait Gallery
The Smithsonian, Washington, DC

The Laterman Collection
New York, NY

The New Britain Museum of Modern Art
New Britain, CT

Awards

Heisey Award

Yale-Norfolk Art School Fellowship

Graduate Assistant Fellowship Yale

50 Best Books Award – A.I.G.A.

Printing for Commerce – A.I.G.A.

Society for World Literacy

Design in Glass – Corning Glass

Simpson Fellowship – Amherst

Art Directors Club of New York

50 Best Ads – A.I.G.A.

Society of Illustrators

New York Employing Printers

Lithographers & Printers National Association

Commemorating the Warsaw Ghetto Uprising

Typmundus 20

American Television Commercials Festival

Society of Publications Designers

Award of Distinctive Merit

Trademarks U.S.A.

International Poster Competition

American Poster 64

A.I.A. Medal

Work Shown at

Museum of Modern Art

Brooklyn Museum

Springfield Art Museum

Pennsylvania University

Wesleyan College

Mead Art Museum - Amherst

Smith College Art Museum

Cooper Union

Kansas City School of Art

University of Indiana

Minneapolis School of Art

Maine State University

Typmundus 20

American Federation of Arts

New York Art Directors Club

A.I.G.A.

Tremaine Gallery at the The Hotchkiss School

The QCC Art Gallery, The City University of NY

The Bellarmine Museum at Fairfield University

Thomas J. Walsh Gallery at Fairfield University

Film Title Design

Bananas *(Woody Allen)*

Everything You Wanted to Know About Sex *(Woody Allen)*

Sleeper *(Woody Allen)*

Little Big Man *(Elliot Erwitt)*

Gladys Knight and the Pips *(Bill Parrott)*

Contributing Designer for the Following Publications

Time Magazine

U.S. News and World Report

Fortune Magazine

CA Magazine *(Cancer Society Journal)*

Impact 21

Maine Magazine

Beverage World

Beverage Aisle

Money Magazine

Financial World

One Magazine *(Catholic Near East Welfare Association)*

Illustrations/Posters

Gorbaty's work as an illustrator has been included in countless magazines, annual reports, brochures, advertisements and numerous children's books. He has also designed posters for such clients as Museum of Modern Art, Walker Art Institute, The Smithsonian and Hoffman–LaRoche Ltd.

Bibliography

Print Making with a Sponn, Reinhold, 1960

Printmaking Methods Old and New, MacMillan Co. 1959

Shabat Radiance
30" x 40"
Oil on Canvas
2010

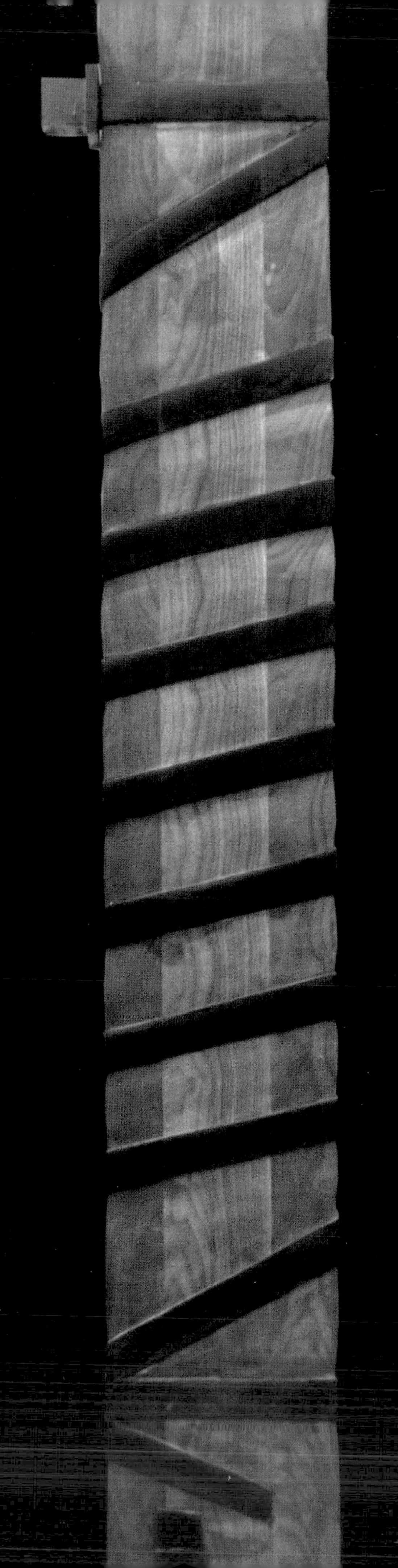

Tvillum

72" x 10" x 2"

Walnut

2010